MW01155093

Time for Korean

Book 2

Time for Korean

Book 2

Revised Edition

Inshil Choe Yoon

Basic Korean for
Young Learners

Hollym

Elizabeth, NJ·Seoul

Time for Korean (Book 2)
Basic Korean for Young Learners

Copyright © 2009
by Inshil Choe Yoon

All rights reserved.
No part of this book may be reproduced in any form
without the prior written permission of the author and the publisher.

Originally published as "Beginner's Korean 나미, 안녕? 2"
© 2003 by Inshil Choe Yoon
Revised edition, 2009
by Hollym International Corp.
18 Donald Place, Elizabeth, New Jersey 07208, USA
Phone 908 353 1655   **Fax** 908 353 0255
http://www.hollym.com

 Hollym

Published simultaneously in Korea
by Hollym Corp., Publishers
13-13 Gwancheol-dong, Jongno-gu, Seoul 110-111, Korea
Phone +82 2 734 5087   **Fax** +82 2 730 8192
http://www.hollym.co.kr   **e-Mail** info@hollym.co.kr

ISBN: 978-1-56591-189-5
Library of Congress Control Number: 2006926995

Printed in Korea

Contents

Preface

During the last decade Korean language programs have been introduced in secondary and primary schools in the United States of America, Australia and New Zealand. While the number and the backgrounds of students learning in the schools vary, one of the common difficulties in teaching the Korean language seems to be acquiring resources that suit the needs of both students and teachers. This book has been developed to cover some of the urgent needs in Korean language teaching at primary and intermediate schools in New Zealand and in other English-speaking countries.

This book is the second of two textbooks of the Korean language designed for beginners at upper primary and intermediate school levels. Based on communicative approach, this book aims at fostering students' skills of listening and speaking Korean through various stimulating activities as well as learning relevant aspects of Korean culture. The twelve units in the book can be covered over a term if Korean is taught for two periods a week; if taught for one period a week, this book can be used over two terms. The units are divided into small sections so that part of a unit can be used for a shorter teaching space, and yet still provide a wholesome lesson.

Each unit consists of either two or three sets of a dialog and an oral task, songs or chants, role-play, word checking, culture note, a review and games. They are task-oriented and integrated for step-by-step Korean language learning with relevant audio input from a compact disk. Romanization of the Korean alphabet is provided in oral tasks and in most other sections. It is advised, however, to listen to the CD for accurate pronunciation of Korean words.

The structure of each unit is as follows:

Look and Listen is a contextualized unit dialog. It is followed by **Let's Talk**, an oral task. After acquiring the pattern of the conversation through aural and visual aids, students are encouraged to make their own dialog related to their class situation.

Each set of dialog and oral task is followed by one or more relevant activities such as **Let's Sing, Let's Chant, Let's Role-play** and **Let's Do It**. These activities are designed to enhance students' listening and speaking skills further.

Culture Note is designed not only to introduce students to Korean culture but also to provide them with activities related to aspects of Korean culture.

Listen and Check, with its aural and visual presentation, provides students with an opportunity to check important phrases or words in each unit.

Let's Review, made up of oral and written tasks based on the dialog provides the learners with further opportunity for review.

Let's Play a Game, inserted after each unit, offers a fun activity that will further enrich spoken language learning experience in the classroom.

Check List is designed to provide students' active preparation of lessons and to aid students in self-monitoring.

Answers and **List of Words and Phrases** will also aid them for their self-assessment and active language use.

Many tasks and challenges lie ahead in developing Korean language programs in secondary and primary schools. I sincerely hope that this book and its accompanying CD will contribute to the enhancement of Korean language programs everywhere.

Acknowledgments

Many people helped me in the development and publication of this textbook. My most sincere gratitude goes to Mrs. Sun Hee Kim and Mrs. Jung Hee Lee for their work in the early stages. Their experience, especially of teaching Korean language to students of this age, made a great contribution toward this book.

I would like to thank the teachers of Korean language in intermediate and secondary schools in New Zealand, especially Pauline Dick, Rosa Lee, Inhee Lee, Eunhee Kim, Young-Sook Kim and Narae Kang for their valuable feedback and suggestions. I thank Lynn Williams for passing me her earlier work for reference.

My gratitude goes to Mr. Ernie Warren and Mrs. Hazel Warren for proofreading the manuscript and music. I am also grateful to Mrs. Hui Jeong Yi and Chloe Lee for their generous help.

I would also like to thank Jeanette McKerchar for recording and editing the CD, Solomon park for the recorded dialogs, Yeonhee Ji and James Koo for the songs, Helen Park for accompaniment and Jae Hoon Kim for recording the songs.

I am grateful to my parents and brothers. I thank Mrs. Jan Westwood, who helped me start the path of language teaching, and the Birkenhead Play Centre parents, who generously shared their lives in working with children. I thank all the colleagues in the School of Asian Studies of The University of Auckland, especially those with whom I have been teaching the Korean language and culture. Finally, I would like to thank Renee Marie for her feedback, and Annabelle, Frances, Caroline, Albert and Hong-key for their encouragement and support.

Inshil Choe Yoon

Unit 01

누구예요?
Who is it?

••• Let's Talk

You are visiting a friend's house. Knock on the door. When asked who you are, introduce yourself.

"누구예요?"
nuguyeyo

"이안이에요."
ianieyo

"어서 오세요."
eoseo oseyo

"안녕하세요?"
annyeonghaseyo

01 누구예요? Who is it?

가족 | Family
gajok

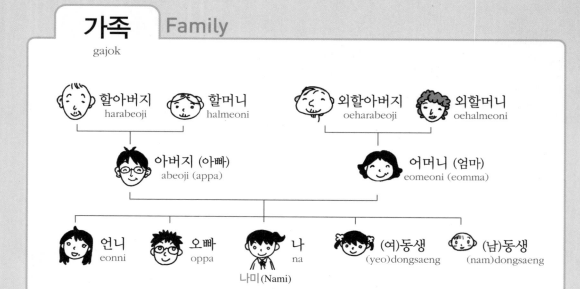

할아버지
harabeoji

할머니
halmeoni

외할아버지
oeharabeoji

외할머니
oehalmeoni

아버지 (아빠)
abeoji (appa)

어머니 (엄마)
eomeoni (eomma)

언니
eonni

오빠
oppa

나
na

나미 (Nami)

(여)동생
(yeo)dongsaeng

(남)동생
(nam)dongsaeng

In the old days, Koreans used to live together as one big family, with grandparents, uncles and aunts from the father's side all under one roof. Nowadays, most families are much smaller and are made up only by parents and children.

Koreans avoid calling their elders by name. Family terms are used within the family. When children call their younger brothers and sisters, they call them by their names. Adults call children by their names, too.

- What are the different points in calling family members between you and Korean children?

••• Let's Role-play

누구예요?

nuguyeyo

Imagine that all the girls in the class are Nami. Point to each person in the family tree and ask the girls nearby who the person is.

누구예요?
nuguyeyo

오빠예요.
oppayeyo
This is my older brother.

Look and Listen 2

••• Let's Talk

Imagine that your partner is either your younger brother, younger sister or your friend. When your group asks you who he/she is, introduce him/her to them.

"얘는 누구예요?"
yaeneun nuguyeyo

"동생이에요. / 친구예요."
dongsaengieyo   chinguyeyo

"이름이 뭐예요?"
ireumi mwoyeyo

"주디예요."
judiyeyo

누구예요?
nuguyeyo

A: 누구예요? Who is this person?
nuguyeyo

B: 동생이에요.
dongsaengieyo

A: 이름이 뭐예요? What is his name?
ireumi mwoyeyo

C: 팀이에요.
timieyo

A: 어서 오세요. Welcome!
eoseo oseyo

C: 안녕하세요?
annyeonghaseyo

A: 누구예요?
nuguyeyo

B: 친구예요.
chinguyeyo

A: 이름이 뭐예요?
ireumi mwoyeyo

C: 빌리(Billy)예요.
billiyeyo

A: 어서 오세요.
eoseo oseyo

C: 안녕하세요?
annyeonghaseyo

나미 어머니
nami eomeoni

나미 할아버지
nami harabeoji

나미 할머니
nami halmeoni

••• Let's Talk

Point to the people above and ask your partner who they are.

"이분은 누구예요?"
ibuneun nuguyeyo

"나미 아버지예요."
nami abeojiyeyo

••• Let's Role-play

이분은 / 얘는 누구예요?
ibuneun   yaeneun nuguyeyo

Imagine that all the boys in the class are Ian.
Point to each person in the photograph and
ask the boys nearby who the person is.

이분은 누구예요?
ibuneun nuguyeyo

누나예요.
nunayeyo
This is my older sister.

이름이 뭐예요?
ireumi mwoyeyo

줄리아예요.
julliayeyo

이안 가족 사진
ian gajok sajin

Ian's family photograph

아버지 abeoji 존 (John)			어머니 eomeoni 제인 (Jane)	
누나 nuna 줄리아 (Julia)	형 hyeong 마이클 (Michael)	나 na 이안 (Ian)	(여)동생 (yeo)dongsaeng 주디 (Judy)	(남)동생 (nam)dongsaeng 팀 (Tim)

Let's Do it

Show your own family photograph and introduce your family as Songmin does below.

우리 가족이에요.

uri gajogieyo

This is my family.

아빠하고 엄마하고 저예요.

appahago eommahago jeoyeyo

Father, mother and me.

저는 학생이에요.

jeoneun haksaengieyo

I am a student.

When Koreans talk about their family members and some other objects, they use "우리 (uri, we/our)" in front of these words, such as "우리 아버지 (abeoji, father)," "우리 가족 (gajok, family)," "우리 집 (jip, house)," "우리 선생님 (seonsaengnim, teacher)," "우리 학교 (hakgyo, school)" and "우리 나라 (nara, country)." Children call their father "아빠 (appa)" and their mother "엄마 (eomma)."

 ## Listen and Check

Listen carefully to the following words.

1. 아버지
abeoji

2. 어머니
eomeoni

3. 할아버지
harabeoji

4. 할머니
halmeoni

5. 남동생
namdongsaeng

••• **Let's Do it** Match the picture with the word that is read out.

a. ☐   b. ☐   c. ☐   d. ☐   e. ☐

Let's Review

1. Complete Nami's family tree by choosing the right words provided below while saying who they are.

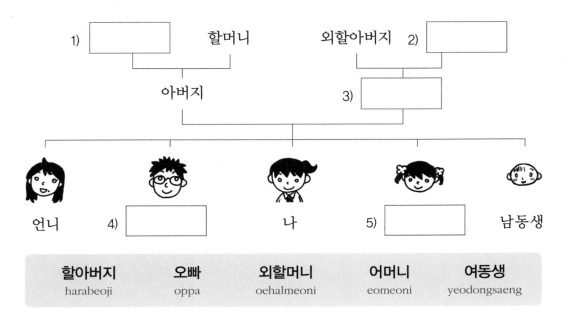

1) ___	할머니	외할아버지	2) ___
아버지		3) ___	
언니	4) ___	나	5) ___	남동생

| 할아버지 | 오빠 | 외할머니 | 어머니 | 여동생 |
| harabeoji | oppa | oehalmeoni | eomeoni | yeodongsaeng |

2. Pepper is asking who the following people are. Answer him by giving their name and profession.

누구예요?

1) 송민(Songmin)이에요.
_____이에요.

2) 루치아노 파바로티(Luciano Pavarotti)   3) 니콜 키드먼(Nicole Kidman)

_____ . _____ .   _____ . _____ .

| 오페라 가수 | 학생 | 영화배우 |
| opera gasu | haksaeng | yeonghwabaeu |

Let's Play a Game "누구하고 누구예요?" Who are they?
nuguhago nuguyeyo

▪ **Aim**: To find out who has moved from their original seat

▪ **Method**: Ask a student to leave the class by saying "나가세요 (nagaseyo)." While he/she is out, two students in the classroom swap seats. Ask the student to come back in, "들어오세요 (deureooseyo)," and start chanting or singing "누구예요? (nuguyeyo)" The student comes in and has to say who swapped seats.

 Let's Chant
TR 03

누구하고 누구예요?
nuguhago nuguyeyo

누구예요? 누구예요? 누구하고 누구예요?
nuguyeyo   nuguyeyo   nuguhago nuguyeyo

나미예요. 이안이에요. 나미하고 이안이에요.
namiyeyo   ianieyo   namihago ianieyo

 Optional Addition
TR 03

If his/her answer is right, the class chants or sings:

맞았어요. 맞았어요.
majasseoyo   majasseoyo
You've done it right.

잘 했어요. 잘 했어요.
jal haesseoyo   jal haesseoyo
You've done it well.

If his/her answer is wrong, the class chants or sings:

틀렸어요. 틀렸어요.
teullyeosseoyo teullyeosseoyo
You've done it wrong.

다시 한 번 해 보세요.
dasi han beon hae boseyo
Try it once more.

* This was developed from a game that Mrs. Lynn Williams introduced to Korean classes.

Unit 02

몇 살이에요?
How old are you?

🎧 TR 04 **Look and Listen 1**

1	하나 hana	2	둘 dul	3	셋 set	4	넷 net
5	다섯 daseot	6	여섯 yeoseot	7	일곱 ilgop	8	여덟 yeodeol
9	아홉 ahop	10	열 yeol	11	열하나 yeolhana	12	열둘 yeoldul
13	열셋 yeolset	14	열넷 yeollet	15	열다섯 yeoldaseot	16	열여섯 yeollyeoseot
17	열일곱 yeorilgop	18	열여덟 yeolleodeol	19	열아홉 yeorahop	20	스물 seumul

30	40	50	60	70	80	90	100
서른 seoreun	마흔 maheun	쉰 swin	예순 yesun	일흔 ilheun	여든 yeodeun	아흔 aheun	백 baek

••• **Let's Do it**

Count from 1 to 12 in groups of four numbers.

"1 2 3 4" "5 6 7 8" "9 10 11 12"

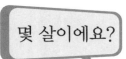

몇 살이에요?

열한 살이에요.

저는
아홉 살이에요.

한 살	두 살	세 살	네 살
han sal	du sal	se sal	ne sal
다섯 살	여섯 살	일곱 살	여덟 살
daseot sal	yeoseot sal	ilgop sal	yeodeol sal
아홉 살	열 살	열한 살	열두 살
ahop sal	yeol sal	yeolhan sal	yeoldu sal

•• Let's Talk

Ask five people how old they are and respond to their answer.

"몇 살이에요?"   **"열한 살이에요."**   **"저는 아홉 살이에요."**
myeot sarieyo   yeolhan sarieyo   jeoneun ahop sarieyo

* If your age is the same as that of the person asked, say "저도 (jeodo)" instead of "저는 (jeoneun)."

 Let's Sing   **"생일 축하합니다"**
saengil chukhahamnida

TR 04

♪ 생일 축하합니다.   생일 축하합니다.
    saengil chukhahamnida   saengil chukhahamnida

   사랑하는 나미/이안 씨, 생일 축하합니다.
   saranghaneun nami   ian ssi   saengil chukhahamnida

Koreans celebrate their birthdays with family and friends. Some birthdays are special: the first year, 돌 (dol), and the sixtieth year, 환갑 (hwangap). On the first birthday, a child wears the traditional Korean costume, 한복 (hanbok), and is seated in front of a table, on the top of which is mostly food, but there are also books, brush, thread, uncooked rice and money. Family and guests are eager to watch which object the child picks up. It is thought that whatever object the child picks up first predicts his or her fortune: if the child picks up a book or a brush, he/she is most likely to become a scholar; if the child picks up a bundle of thread, he/she will live a long life; if the child picks up rice or money, he/she will be rich.

On parents' sixtieth birthday, families express their happiness and thanks to them by offering a big feast. The parents sit in the middle of a big table with layers of food and receive their children who bow on their knees.

In the past these two birthdays have been very joyful occasions: many babies died before their first birthday, and few people lived to be sixty years old. Nowadays, most babies reach the first birthday and many people live to be older than sixty, but Koreans still celebrate these occasions in a special manner.

- What do you find most interesting about Koreans' celebration of special birthdays? Why?
- What are some special birthdays in your country?
- How do people celebrate them?

Look and Listen 3

••• Let's Talk

Find out the number of boys and girls in your class by counting them, and then complete the box below.

"몇 명이에요?"
myeot myeongieyo

"한 명,   두 명,   세 명,   네 명,
han myeong   du myeong   se myong   ne myong

다섯 명,   여섯 명 ... ———— 명이에요."
daseot myeong yeoseot myeong   myeongieyo

남학생 namhaksaeng		명
여학생 yeohaksaeng		명

 **Let's Chant**

TR 05

꼬마 인디안 열 명
kkoma indian yeol myeong

꼬마	인디안	한 명,	두 명,	세 명
kkoma	indian	han myeong	du myeong	se myong

꼬마	인디안	네 명,	다섯 명,	여섯 명
kkoma	indian	ne myeong	daseot myeong	yeoseot myong

꼬마	인디안	일곱 명,	여덟 명,	아홉 명
kkoma	indian	ilgop myeong	yeodeol myeong	ahop myong

열 명	있어요.
yeol myeong	isseoyo

 Let's Sing "꼬마 인디안 열 명"
kkoma indian yeol myeong

TR 05

Tune : Traditional
Words: Inshil Choe Yoon

꼬 마 인 디 안 한 명 두 명 세 명 꼬 마 인 디 안 네 명 다 섯 명 여 섯 명

꼬 마 인 디 안 일 곱 명 여 덟 명 아 홉 명 열 명 있 어 요

Listen and Check

TR 05

Listen carefully to the following words.

1.
1
hana

2.
5
daseot

3.
3
set

4.
2
dul

5.
7
ilgop

••• **Let's Do it** Enter the number that is read out.

a. ☐   b. ☐   c. ☐   d. ☐   e. ☐

Let's Review

1. Connect the numbers and words.

1	2	3	4	5	6	7	8
●	●	●	●	●	●	●	●
●	●	●	●	●	●	●	●
둘	하나	셋	넷	다섯	여섯	여덟	일곱
dul	hana	set	net	daseot	yeoseot	yeodeol	ilgop

2. Connect the questions with the right answers.

1) 몇 살이에요?
   myeot sarieyo

   a) 열 살이에요.
      yeol sarieyo

2) 가족이 몇 명이에요?
   gajogi myeot myeongieyo

   b) 세 명이에요.
      se myeongieyo

3) 누구하고 누구예요?
   nuguhago nuguyeyo

   c) 아빠하고 엄마하고 나예요.
      appahago eommahago nayeyo

3. Answer Snowy's questions.

가족이 몇 명이에요?

몇 살이에요?

4. Complete the following into your own counting song by choosing the word that you like.

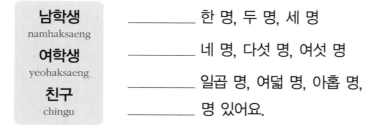

남학생
namhaksaeng

여학생
yeohaksaeng

친구
chingu

_____ 한 명, 두 명, 세 명

_____ 네 명, 다섯 명, 여섯 명

_____ 일곱 명, 여덟 명, 아홉 명,

_____ 명 있어요.

Let's Play a Game "하나, 둘, 셋, 꽥!" One, Two, Three, Quack!
hana dul set kkwaek

▪ **Aim**: To listen to and count the numbers from 1 except for the multiples of 4

▪ **Method**: The class sits in a circle. The first person calls out "하나 (hana 1)," the next person "둘 (dul 2)," and the next "셋 (set 3)." The next person says "꽥 (kkwaek)" instead of calling out "넷 (net 4)." The person after that calls out "다섯 (daseot 5)," and so on. The student whose turn it is at the multiples of 4 is expected to say "꽥 (kkwaek)." Students who don't remember the rule are out. Those who stay in after five rounds of the game are the winners.

TR 05

하나, 둘, 셋, 꽥!
hana dul set kkwaek

하나, 둘, 셋, 꽥!
hana dul set kkwaek

다섯, 여섯, 일곱, 꽥!
daseot yeoseot ilgop kkwaek!

아홉, 열, 열하나, 꽥!
ahop yeol yeolhana kkwaek

열셋, 열넷, 열다섯, 꽥!
yeolset yeollet yeoldaseot kkwaek

* You can say "꿀꿀 (kkulkkul oink-oink)" instead of saying "꽥 (kkwaek quack)".

Unit
03

어디에서 왔어요?
Where are you from?

Look and Listen 1
TR 06

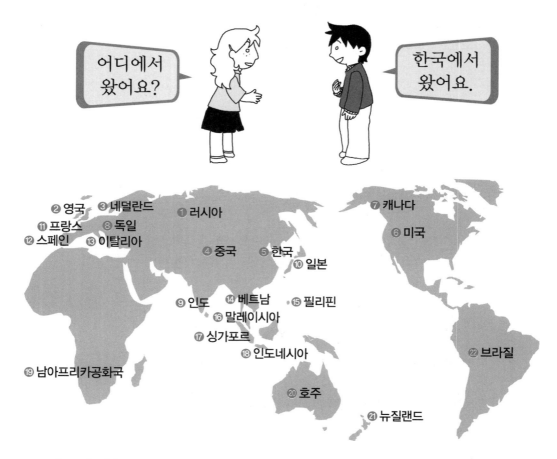

- 어디에서 왔어요?
- 한국에서 왔어요.

- ② 영국
- ③ 네덜란드
- ❶ 러시아
- ⑪ 프랑스
- ⑧ 독일
- ⑫ 스페인
- ⑬ 이탈리아
- ④ 중국
- ⑤ 한국
- ⑩ 일본
- ⑦ 캐나다
- ⑥ 미국
- ⑨ 인도
- ⑭ 베트남
- ⑮ 필리핀
- ⑯ 말레이시아
- ⑰ 싱가포르
- ⑱ 인도네시아
- ⑲ 남아프리카공화국
- ⑳ 호주
- ㉑ 뉴질랜드
- ㉒ 브라질

••• Let's Talk

Ask three people where (which country) they are from.

"어디에서 왔어요?"
eodieseo wasseoyo

"한국에서 왔어요."
hangugeseo wasseoyo

Let's Chant

TR 07

어디에서 왔어요?
eodieseo wasseoyo

어디에서 왔어요?
eodieseo wasseoyo

어디에서 왔어요?
eodieseo wasseoyo

한국에서 왔어요.
hangugeseo wasseoyo

한국에서 왔어요.
hangugeseo wasseoyo

어디에서 왔어요?
eodieseo wasseoyo

어디에서 왔어요?
eodieseo wasseoyo

영국에서 왔어요.
yeonggugeseo wasseoyo

영국에서 왔어요.
yeonggugeseo wasseoyo

Let's Sing   "어디에서 왔어요?"
eodieseo wasseoyo

TR 07

Tune : Traditional
Words: Inshil Choe Yoon

어 디 에 서 왔 어 요 어 디 에 서 왔 어 요

한 국 에 서 왔 , 어 요 한 국 에 서 왔 어 요
영 국 에 서 왔 어 요 영 국 에 서 왔 어 요

Let's Sing with Actions

Divide the class into two groups. Groups A and B line up facing each other. The group A chants or sings the first line while skipping toward a member of the group B.
When the group B chants or sings the second line and skips forward, the group A skips backwards.

Look and Listen 2

한국 어디에서 왔어요?

서울에서 왔어요.

평양 Pyeongyang
서울 Seoul
Incheon 인천
수원 Suwon
대전 Daejeon
대구 Daegu
광주 Gwangju
부산 Busan

중국 베이징 (Beijing) beijing

미국 워싱턴 (Washington) wosingteon

호주 캔버라 (Canberra) kaenbeora

뉴질랜드 웰링턴 (Wellington) wellingteon

싱가포르 싱가포르 (Singapore) singgaporeu

••• Let's Talk

Ask three classmates who have come from overseas which part of the country they came from.

"한국 어디에서 왔어요?"
hanguk eodieseo wasseoyo

"서울에서 왔어요."
seoureseo wasseoyo

Listen and Check

Listen carefully to the following words.

1. 한국 hanguk
2. 미국 miguk
3. 중국 jungguk
4. 호주 hoju
5. 뉴질랜드 nyujillaendeu

••• Let's Do it Match the picture with the word that is read out.

a. ☐   b. ☐   c. ☐   d. ☐   e. ☐

서울
Seoul

The capital of Korea

Seoul has been the capital and the center of business of Korea for more than 600 years. The old city of Seoul was enclosed by a city wall, but citizens could move in and out of the city through the city gates. The East Gate, 동대문 (dongdaemun), and the South Gate, 남대문 (namdaemun), still remain. Gyeongbokgung Palace, 경복궁 (gyeongbokgung), is the most famous palace in Seoul because Korean kings, including King Sejong the Great, 세종대왕 (sejongdaewang), lived and ruled Korea from there. We can now visit all the palaces because they are open to the public. The Korean president lives in the Blue House, 청와대 (cheongwadae), which is close to Gyeongbokgung Palace.

In the 20th century, the city has grown in all directions, especially to the south of the Han River, 한강 (hangang). About 10 million people (2008 estimate) are living in the city of Seoul. High-rise buildings and apartments are seen everywhere in Seoul. There are over twenty bridges for cars, buses, trains and subways over the Han River. Subway lines in Seoul cover 304 km, the 4th longest in the world. Subways are the fastest (90km/hour) and most convenient way to travel in Seoul. They run every 4-6 minutes from 5:30 a.m. to midnight. Traveling by subway is the most popular in Seoul: in 2004, 35.8% of travel within the city was by subway.

Seoul hosted the 1988 Olympic Games and was one of the cities that hosted FIFA World Cup soccer matches in 2002. The tournament was co-hosted by Korea and Japan.

● Which place in Seoul do you want to visit or know more about? Why?
● What famous places have you read about or visited?

1. Answer Snowy's question.

어디에서
왔어요?

2. Draw lines to make correct sentences.

1) 팬더는   ●
  paendeoneun

     ● a) 뉴질랜드에서 왔어요.
        nyujillaendeueseo wasseoyo

2) 캥거루는   ●
  kaenggeoruneun

     ● b) 호주에서 왔어요.
        hojueseo wasseoyo

3) 키위는   ●
  kiwineun

     ● c) 중국에서 왔어요.
        junggugeseo wasseoyo

3. Fill in the blanks.

영국	캐나다	아프리카	호주
yeongguk	kaenada	apeurika	hoju

1) ＿＿＿에서 왔어요.

2) ＿＿＿에서 왔어요.

3) ＿＿＿에서 왔어요.

4) ＿＿＿에서 왔어요.

••• Let's Role-play

"똑똑" "누구예요?"
ttokttok   nuguyeyo

Divide the class into groups of 2-4 people. Each group acts as one of the animals shown below. Choose the name of the animal and the place of origin (country and city). Start a conversation by knocking at an imaginary door.

Other groups

누구예요?
nuguyeyo

이름이 뭐예요?
ireumi mwoyeyo

어디에서 왔어요?
eodieseo wasseoyo

뉴질랜드 어디에서 왔어요?
nyujillaendeu eodieseo wasseoyo

어서 오세요.
eoseo oseyo

Group A

똑똑
ttokttok

키위예요.
kiwiyeyo

키리(Kiri)예요. / 존이에요.
kiriyeyo   jonieyo

뉴질랜드에서 왔어요.
nyujillaendeueseo wasseoyo

오클랜드에서 왔어요.
okeullaendeueseo wasseoyo

안녕하세요?
annyeonghaseyo

팬더

코끼리

캥거루

펭귄

버팔로

Unit 04

어떻게 지내요?

How have you been?

🎧 Look and Listen 1

TR 08

••• Let's Talk

Ask your group members how they are getting on. If someone is sick, ask where it hurts.

"어떻게 지내요?"
eotteoke jinaeyo

"잘 지내요. / 그저 그래요. / 아파요."
jal jinaeyo   geujeo geuraeyo   apayo

"어디가 아파요?"
eodiga apayo

"머리가 아파요. / 눈이 아파요."
meoriga apayo   nuni apayo

머리	어깨	무릎	발	무릎	발
meori	eokkae	mureup	bal	mureup	bal
머리	어깨	무릎	발	무릎	발
meori	eokkae	mureup	bal	mureup	bal
머리	어깨	발	무릎	발	
meori	eokkae	bal	mureup	bal	
머리	어깨	무릎	귀	코	귀
meori	eokkae	mureup	gwi	ko	gwi

Sing along with your class touching your head, shoulders, knees, and feet. You can change the name of body parts.

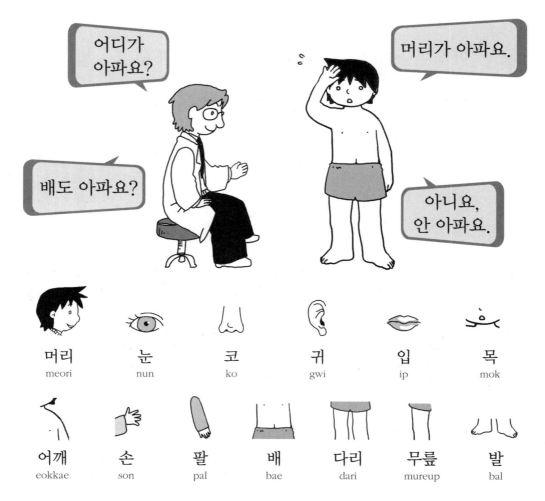

머리	눈	코	귀	입	목
meori	nun	ko	gwi	ip	mok

어깨	손	팔	배	다리	무릎	발
eokkae	son	pal	bae	dari	mureup	bal

••• Let's Talk

Find out which body part of your partner hurts.

"어디가 아파요?"
eodiga apayo

"머리가 아파요."
meoriga apayo

"배도 아파요?"
baedo apayo

"아니요, 안 아파요."
aniyo an apayo

••• **Let's Talk**

It is time to say good-bye. In pairs, one person acts as a patient and the other a doctor. The patient goes toward a door, saying "안녕히 계세요 (annyeonghi gyeseyo good-bye)." The doctor says, "안녕히 가세요 (annyeonghi gaseyo good-bye)" to the patient.

"안녕히 계세요."   "안녕히 가세요."
annyeonghi gyeseyo   annyeonghi gaseyo

한국 가정 방문   Visiting a Korean home
hanguk gajeong bangmun

When people visit their friends and relatives in Korea, they often take fruit with them. Koreans welcome visitors with great hospitality. All members of a family come out of their rooms to greet visitors. If the visitors are not staying for a meal, they are given fruit or cookies and a cup of tea. Korean children are encouraged to be polite. When the visitors leave, all members of the family come out of the house to say goodbye, "안녕히 가세요 (annyeonghi gaseyo)." It is common to see Koreans who live in high-rise apartments come down by elevator to the ground floor to see their guests off. It is also common to give the guests some kind of present to take home.

● What is different about the way Korean children receive visitors?
● What is similar between you and Korean children?

••• Let's Role-play

어디가 아파요?
eodiga apayo

One student is a doctor and the rest of the class are patients. When the doctor welcomes and asks a patient whether a certain part of the body hurts, the patient touches that part and answers. If the patient touches the wrong part, he/she becomes the doctor and welcomes the next patient.

의사 선생님 uisa seonsaengnim	환자 hwanja
어서 오세요. eseo oseyo	의사 선생님, 안녕하세요? uisa seonsaengnim annyeonghaseyo
안녕하세요? 앉으세요. annyeonghaseyo anjeuseyo	네. ne
어디가 아파요? eodiga apayo	머리가 아파요. meoriga apayo
목도 아파요? mokdo apayo	네, 목도 아파요. ne mokdo apayo
배도 아파요? baedo apayo	아니요, 안 아파요. aniyo an apayo
많이 쉬세요. mani swiseyo	네. ne
안녕히 가세요. annyeonghi gaseyo	안녕히 계세요. annyeonhi gyeseyo

🎧 TR 09 Listen and Check

Listen carefully to the following words.

1. 눈
nun

2. 코
ko

3. 머리
meori

4. 귀
gwi

••• **Let's Do it** Match the picture with the word that is read out.

a. ☐   b. ☐   c. ☐   d. ☐

1. Connect the questions with the right answers.

    1) 어떻게 지내요?   ●   ● a) 잘 지내요.
       eotteoke jinaeyo   jal jinaeyo

    2) 어디가 아파요?   ●   ● b) 아니요, 배가 아파요.
       eodiga apayo   aniyo baega apayo

    3) 발이 아파요?   ●   ● c) 손이 아파요.
       bari apayo   soni apayo

2. Draw your body and link the part of the body to the words.

머리
meori

어깨
eokkae

배
bae

팔
pal

손
son

다리
dari

무릎
mureup

발
bal

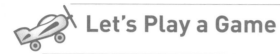

Let's Play a Game "코코코코 눈!"
ko ko ko ko nun

• **Aim**: To show the body part which has been called out

• **Method**: A student pats his/her nose with a pointer, saying "코코코코 (kokokoko)" and then calls out the name of another body part but touches a different part of the body. The class must touch the new body part which has been called out and not the part that the student touches. The first person who fails to do so becomes "it."

Let's Chant
TR 09

코코코코 눈!
ko ko ko ko nun

코코코코 눈!
ko ko ko ko nun

코코코코 입!
ko ko ko ko ip

코코코코 귀!
ko ko ko ko gwi

코코코코 머리!
ko ko ko ko meori

Unit 05

어디에 가요?
Where are you going?

Look and Listen 1

TR 10

학교	집	병원	수영장
hakgyo	jip	byeongwon	suyeongjang

••• Let's Talk

Ask five people where they are going (after school).

"어디에 가요?"   "가게에 가요."
eodie gayo   gagee gayo

Let's Chant

TR 11

타잔(Tarzan) 씨, 타잔 씨, 어디에 가요?
tajan ssi tajan ssi eodie gayo

타잔 씨, 타잔 씨, 어디에 가요?
tajan ssi tajan ssi eodie gayo

가게에 가요. 가게에 가요.
gagee gayo   gagee gayo

스노이 씨, 스노이 씨, 어디에 가요?
seunoi ssi seunoi ssi eodie gayo

학교에 가요. 학교에 가요.
hakgyoe gayo   hakgyoe gayo

 Let's Sing "타잔 씨, 타잔 씨, 어디에 가요?"
tajan ssi tajan ssi eodie gayo

TR 11

Tune : Traditional
Words: Inshil Choe Yoon

타 잔　씨 타 잔 씨　어 디　에 가 —요　가 게　에 가 요　가 게　에 가 요
스노이　씨 스노이씨　어 디　에 가 —요　학 교　에 가 요　학 교　에 가 요

 **Let's Sing with Actions**

Divide the class into two groups. Groups A and B line up and face each other. The group A marches forward, asking where a member of the group B is going, to the tune of the first line. The person whose name has been called out marches forward and says where he/she is going to the tune of the second line while the group A marches backwards. The group A marches forward again, asking where another member of the group B is going, to which the member then answers. The groups A and B then switch roles.

학교, 교실   Schools and classrooms
hakgyo   gyosil

Schools in Korea are often big buildings that have a large open area, 운동장 (undongjang), out front. This *undongjang* is sandy earth and is used for assemblies for the whole school or for sports and games. In a corner of the *undongjang*, there is a playground with junglegyms and bars. A big hall is also used for assemblies and concerts. School buildings are usually more than one story.

Buildings usually have several classrooms on one side and a long corridor on the other side. Because classrooms have windows on both sides, people can look in at classes as they walk along the corridor. Students have their own white slippers with rubber soles that they change into before going into their classrooms. In primary school there are about thirty students in each class. Some rooms are designed for special purposes: science classrooms; resource rooms; kitchen. Lunch is prepared in the kitchen and taken out to classrooms or the lunch room at lunch time. Schools are surrounded by walls and the school grounds are kept clean and safe by a custodian.

- What things are different between your school and Korean schools?
- Why do you think Korean schools are different from your school?
- What things are similar?

우체국	영화관	교회	동물원
ucheguk	yeonghwagwan	gyohoe	dongmurwon

••• Let's Talk

Ask your partner where he/she is going. If you find out that you are going to the same place, suggest that you go together, using "저도 (jeodo)." If not, say where you are going using "저는 (jeoneun)" instead of "저도."

"어디에 가요?"
eodie gayo

"공원에 가요."
gongwone gayo

"저도 공원에 가요."
jeodo gongwone gayo

"같이 가요."
gachi gayo

Look and Listen 3

미국 **샌프란시스코** **로스앤젤리스** **시카고**   캐나다 **토론토** **밴쿠버**
    (San Francisco)   (Los Angeles)   (Chicago)   (Toronto)   (Vancouver)
   saenpeuransisko   loseuaenjelliseu   sikago   toronto   baenkubeo

뉴질랜드 **크라이스트처치** **던이든**   호주 **멜번** **브리스번** **퍼스**
      (Christchurch)   (Dunedin)   (Melbourne)   (Brisbane)   (Perth)
  keuraiseuteucheochi   deonideun   melbeoreun   beuriseubeon   peoseu

••• Let's Talk

Imagine that all of your classmates are going overseas to visit a city. Ask five people where they are going like the examples below.

"어디에 가요?"   "미국에 가요."
    eodie gayo   miguge gayo

"미국 어디에 가요?"   "뉴욕에 가요."
    miguk eodie gayo   nyuyoge gayo

Listen and Check

Listen carefully to the following words.

1.
학교
hakgyo

2.
교회
gyohoe

3.
우체국
ucheguk

4.
수영장
suyeongjang

••• Let's Do it   Match the picture with the word that is read out.

a. ☐   b. ☐   c. ☐   d. ☐

Let's Review

1. Answer Pepper's question.

어디에 가요?

2. Fill in the blanks with words from the box.

공원	영화관	도서관	동물원
gongwon	yeonghwagwan	doseogwan	dongmurwon

1) A: 어디에 가요?
   eodie gayo

   B: 공원에 가요.
   gongwone gayo

   A: 저도 _____에 가요.
   jeodo   e gayo

   B: 같이 가요.
   gachi gayo

2) A: 어디에 가요?
   eodie gayo

   B: 병원에 가요.
   byeongwone gayo

   A: 저는 _____에 가요.
   jeoneun   e gayo

   B: 안녕히 가세요.
   annyeonghi gaseyo

   A: 안녕히 가세요.
   annyeonghi gaseyo

3. Complete the following song by choosing words from the box.

가게	학교	병원
gage	hakgyo	byeongwon
교회	정글	
gyohoe	jeonggeul	

나미 씨, 나미 씨, 어디에 가요?

[   ]에 가요. [   ]에 가요.

아나 씨, 아나 씨, 어디에 가요?

[   ]에 가요. [   ]에 가요.

4. Connect the questions with the right answers.

1) 어디에 가요?   •   • a) 영국에 가요.

2) 영국 어디에 가요?   •   • b) 런던에 가요.

Let's Play a Game "같이 가요!" Let's go together.
gachi gayo

▪ **Aim**: To find out where others are going and to make a suitable response

▪ **Method**: Everybody decides on a place to go. Walk around the classroom and ask a person where he/she is going. If you are going to the same place, say "같이 가요 (gachi gayo)" to suggest that you walk together. If you meet a student or a group of students while the two of you are going to the same place, use "우리도 (urido)" instead of "저도 (jeodo)."

A: 안녕하세요?
   annyeonghaseyo

A: 어디에 가요?
   eodie gayo

A: 저도 가게에 가요.
   jeodo gagee gayo

B: 안녕하세요?
   annyeonghaseyo

B: 가게에 가요.
   gagee gayo

B: 같이 가요!
   gachi gayo

If you find out that you are not going to the same place, say where you are going using "저는 (jeoneun)."

A: 안녕하세요?
   annyeonghaseyo

A: 어디에 가요?
   eodie gayo

A: 저는 가게에 가요.
   jeoneun gagee gayo

A: 안녕히 가세요.
   annyeonghi gaseyo

B: 안녕하세요?
   annyeonghaseyo

B: 공원에 가요.
   gongwone gayo

B: 안녕히 가세요.
   annyeonghi gaseyo

Unit 06

개를 좋아해요?
Do you like dogs?

Look and Listen 1

TR 12

고양이	토끼
goyangi	tokki

물고기
mulgogi

새
sae

••• Let's Talk

Ask five people whether they like animals such as hamsters or guinea pigs or those shown above, and then ask how many they have.

"개를 좋아해요?"
gaereul joahaeyo

"네, 좋아해요."
ne joahaeyo

"개 있어요?"
gae isseoyo

"네, 한 마리 있어요."
ne han mari isseoyo

거미
geomi

파리
pari

모기
mogi

••• Let's Talk

Ask three people whether they like the animals shown above or other animals they may not like.

"뱀을 좋아해요?"
baemeul joahaeyo

"아니요, 안 좋아해요."
aniyo an joahaeyo

"싫어해요."
sireohaeyo

Let's Sing "고양이는 야옹!"
goyangineun yaong

고양이는 야옹! 고양이는 야옹!
goyangineun yaong goyangineun yaong

개는 멍멍! 개는 멍멍!
gaeneun meong-meong gaeneun meong-meong

양은 매애! 양은 매애!
yangeun mae-ae yangeun mae-ae

소는 음매! 소는 음매!
soneun eummae soneun eummae

Tune : Traditional
Words: Inshil Choe Yoon

고 양 이 는 야 옹   고 양 이 는 야 옹   개 는 멍 멍   개 는 멍 멍

양 은 매 애   양 은 매 애   소 는 음 매   소 는 음 매

 Listen and Check

Listen carefully to the following words.

1.
거미
geomi

2.
토끼
tokki

3.
물고기
mulgogi

4.
뱀
baem

5.
다람쥐
daramjwi

•• **Let's Do it** Match the picture with the word that is read out.

a. ☐   b. ☐   c. ☐   d. ☐   e. ☐

토끼 tokki	다람쥐 daramjwi	뱀 baem
소 so	양 yang	새 sae

••• Let's Talk

Ask five people whether they are looking for a certain lost pet.

"고양이를 찾아요?"
goyangireul chajayo

"아니요, 개를 찾아요."
aniyo gaereul chajayo

호랑이, 곰, 단군 A tiger, a bear and Dangun
horangi   gom   dangun

According to the national foundation myth of Korea, Dangun founded Korea in 2333 BC. His mother was a bear that had turned into a woman, and his father was a god.

Once upon a time, Hwanung, a son of the god, Hwanin, wanted very much to live in the human world. Hwanin blessed him by giving him three kingly seals and allowed him to rule the world. Hwanung left heaven, bringing three thousand friends and arrived on top of Mt. Taebaeksan in Korea. Together with the three masters of wind, rain and clouds, he looked after his people very well.

A bear and a tiger living in a cave nearby begged Hwanung to change them into human beings. He gave them a clump of mugwort plant (related to the chrysamthemum) and twenty cloves of garlic. He told them that in order to become human beings, they had to live on these foods for 100 days in the dark cave. They agreed to follow the instructions and ate the plant and garlic.

The bear lived patiently in the dark cave, but the tiger could not stand it and gave up. Only the bear then became a woman. The bear lady wanted to find a person to marry but could not find a suitable man. Hwanung became a man and married her. The bear lady got pregnant and had a son, who was called Dangun. In 2333 BC, Dangun became the first king of the Korean kingdom. He was a wise king and served his people for many years.

● What do you find interesting in the above story? How come?
● What are some myths that you know?

••• Let's Role-play

소를 찾아요?
soreul chajayo

Divide the class into three groups. Each group quietly decides which animal they want to be and which animal they will be looking for. The group A makes the sound of the animal and the other groups ask questions to find out which animal the group A is and which animal it is looking for. The group A can only answer "네 (ne)" or "아니요(aniyo)."

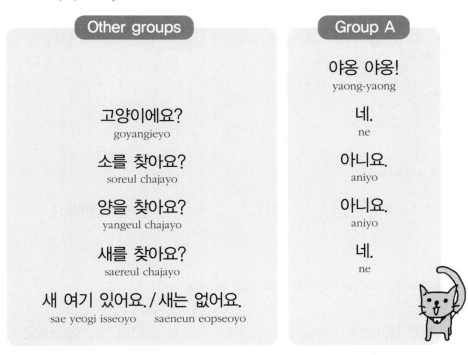

Other groups

고양이에요?
goyangieyo

소를 찾아요?
soreul chajayo

양을 찾아요?
yangeul chajayo

새를 찾아요?
saereul chajayo

새 여기 있어요. / 새는 없어요.
sae yeogi isseoyo   saeneun eopseoyo

Group A

야옹 야옹!
yaong-yaong

네.
ne

아니요.
aniyo

아니요.
aniyo

네.
ne

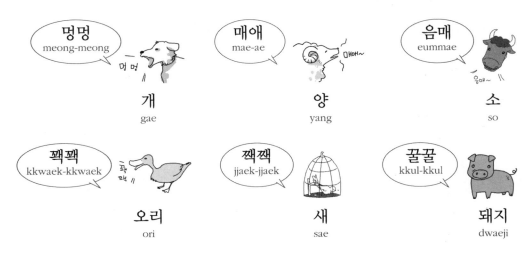

멍멍
meong-meong

개
gae

매애
mae-ae

양
yang

음매
eummae

소
so

꽥꽥
kkwaek-kkwaek

오리
ori

짹짹
jjaek-jjaek

새
sae

꿀꿀
kkul-kkul

돼지
dwaeji

Let's Review

1. Check the boxes that apply to you.

	새 sae	뱀 baem	물고기 mulgogi	거미 geomi
좋아해요 joahaeyo				
싫어해요 sireohaeyo				

2. Fill in the blanks.

저는 ＿＿＿＿＿하고 ＿＿＿＿＿을/를 좋아해요.
jeoneun   hago   eul reul joahaeyo

3. Connect the questions with the right answers.

1) 토끼를 찾아요?   •
    tokkireul chajayo

2) 파리를 좋아해요?   •
    parireul joahaeyo

3) 고양이 있어요?   •
    goyangi isseoyo

4) 몇 마리 있어요?   •
    myeot mari isseoyo

• a) 아니요, 싫어해요.
    aniyo sireohaeyo

• b) 네, 있어요.
    ne isseoyo

• c) 아니요, 개를 찾아요.
    aniyo gaereul chajayo

• d) 두 마리 있어요.
    du mari isseoyo

멍 멍

Let's Play a Game "누구를 찾아요?" Who are you looking for?
nugureul chajayo

• **Aim:** To get the most number of people in your group by giving the correct name of the country of origin of other group members

• **Method:** Divide the class into two equal groups. Both groups decide on a member of the other group whom they would like to have as their own member. The group A skips towards the group B chanting or singing the first and third lines while the group B skips towards the group A chanting or singing the second and fourth lines. If the group B guesses the student's country of the origin correctly, the person whose name was called out and the representative of the group B play "Rock, paper and scissors." The loser joins the winning group. If the group B fails to guess correctly the country of origin of the member called, a member of the group B goes to the group A. The group who has more members after five times of the game is the winner. The first person who fails to so becomes "it."

가위　　　　바위　　　　보
gawi　　　　bawi　　　　bo

TR 13

Let's Sing "누구를 찾아요?"
nugureul chajayo

♪ 누구를 찾아요? (×2)
nugureul chajayo

나미를 찾아요. (×2)
nugureul chajayo

나미는, 나미는 어디에서 왔어요?
namineun namineun eodieseo wasseoyo

한국에서 왔어요. (×2)
hangugeseo wassseoyo

* This was developed from a traditional Korean game, "uri jibe wae wanni."

Unit 07

수영해요?
Do you swim?

 Look and Listen 1
TR 14

수영해요?

네, 수영해요.

아니요, 안 해요.

축구
chukgu

야구
yagu

농구
nonggu

배구
baegu

탁구
takgu

럭비
reokbi

테니스
teniseu

••• Let's Talk

Ask three people whether they play a certain sport.

"수영해요?"
suyeonghaeyo

"네, 수영해요."
ne suyeonghaeyo

"아니요, 안 해요."
aniyo an haeyo

하키
haki

넷볼
netbol

골프
golpeu

••• Let's Talk

Ask three people around you what sports they play.

"무슨 운동 해요?"
museun undong haeyo

"태권도 해요."
taegwondo haeyo

 Let's Chant

TR 15

축구   야구   농구   배구
chukgu   yagu   nonggu   baegu

따라 하세요.
ttara haseyo

Repeat slowly after your teacher, pointing to the pictures on page 54.

축구	야구	농구	배구	탁구	럭비	테니스
chukgu	yago	nonggu	baegu	takgu	reokbi	teniseu

태권도
Taegwondo
Korea's traditional martial art

Taegwondo is a traditional Korean martial art which has been developed for over 2,000 years. Koreans practice *taegwondo* not only for self-defense but also for their moral training.

Nowadays, many Korean school boys and girls learn *taegwondo*. They start with a white belt. As they pass grading tests, they change the belt to yellow, green, blue, red and eventually to black.

Taegwondo was adopted as an official sport at the Sydney Olympic Games in 2000. It is taught and practiced in over one hundred countries, with all instructions in Korean, for example, "시작 (sijak start)," "하나 (hana one)," "둘 (dul two)," "셋 (set three)," "넷 (net four)."

- Why do some people learn martial arts?
- Which martial arts do you practice or know about?

••• Let's Play Charades

무슨 운동 해요?
museun undong haeyo

The class asks "무슨 운동 해요? (museun undong haeyo)" to a student. When the student makes a gesture, the class guesses what sports he/she plays. If the class cannot give the correct answer, the class can go through a list of sports he/she might play, asking, for example, "테니스해요? (teniseuhaeyo)."

1) 무슨 운동 해요?
   museun undong haeyo

2) 테니스해요? 축구해요?
   teniseuhaeyo   chukguhaeyo

Look and Listen 3

TR 15

캠핑을 좋아해요?

아니요, 말타기를 좋아해요.

낚시
naksi

달리기
dalligi

스키
seuki

••• Let's Talk

Ask three people whether they like a certain outdoor activity.

"캠핑을 좋아해요?"
kaempingeul joahaeyo

"아니요, 말타기를 좋아해요."
aniyo maltagireul joahaeyo

 ## Listen and Check

TR 15

Listen carefully to the following words.

1.

축구
chukgu

2.

테니스
teniseu

3.

탁구
takgu

4.

하키
haki

••• **Let's Do it** Match the picture with the word that is read out.

a. ☐   b. ☐   c. ☐   d. ☐

1. Answer Snowy's question.

무슨 운동 해요?

_____하고 _____ 해요.

2. Connect the words to the right pictures and answer the question.

무슨 운동을 좋아해요?

1) 탁구
takgu

2) 달리기
dalligi

3) 말타기
maltagi

4) 태권도
taegwondo

3. Check the right cell.

	야구해요 yaguhaeyo	골프해요 golpeuhaeyo	테니스해요 teniseuhaeyo	농구해요 nongguhaeyo	축구해요 chukguhaeyo
1) 박찬호 (Chan-ho Park)	∨				
2) 앙드레 아가시 (Andre Agassi)					
3) 마이클 조던 (Michael Jordan)					
4) 타이거 우즈 (Tiger Woods)					
5) 데이비드 베컴 (David Beckham)					

Let's Play a Game "수영을 좋아해요." I like swimming.
suyeongeul joahaeyo

- **Aim**: To listen accurately to what sports other people like and to act each out in a limited time

- **Method**: One student stands in front of the classroom. The class gathers behind a line, away from the student. When the student starts chanting the sports that he/she likes to play, while looking away from the class, for example, "수영을 좋아해요 (suyeongeul joahaeyo)," the class approaches him/her with a swimming motion. The class stops approaching before the chanting is over. When the student turns back and finds someone moving, he/she calls out the name of the person, who then becomes "it." If the student, while chanting, was touched by a class member, he/she turns around and chases the class. If the class runs up to the line without being touched, the student starts the game again. If someone is caught, this person becomes "it." He/she stands in front of the class and continues the game by calling out what sport he/she likes playing.

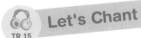 **Let's Chant**

TR 15

수영을 좋아해요.
suyeongeul joahaeyo

수영을 좋아해요.
수영을 좋아해요.
수영을 좋아해요.
수영을 좋아해요.

* This was developed from a traditional Korean game, "il i sam sa o yuk chil pal gu sip."

* Variation: You can change the names of sports with those of animals which you like.

지금 몇 시예요?

What time is it now?

 Look and Listen 1
TR16

지금 몇 시예요?

1:00

한 시예요.

두 시	세 시	네 시	다섯 시
du si	se si	ne si	daseot si

6:00	7:00	8:00	9:00
여섯 시	일곱 시	여덟 시	아홉 시
yeoseot si	ilgop si	yeodeol si	ahop si

••• Let's Talk

Point out the clocks above and ask your partner what time it is.

"지금 몇 시예요?"
jigeum myeot siyeyo

"한 시예요."
han siyeyo

학교 생활   A day at school

hakgyo saenghwal

Students in Korea arrive at school by nine o'clock in the morning. After two periods of study, every student in elementary school is given a carton of milk to drink.

Elementary school students do not bring their lunch from home. At lunch hour, students in senior years take turns bringing a lunch cart loaded with food for the whole class from the kitchen to their classroom. Two or three students serve lunch while the rest of the class line up for their turn. In junior classes, mother helpers serve food. The menu changes every day and students can decide on the amount of food that they want to eat. After finishing the meal, the students who served lunch take the cart and food trays back to the kitchen. Then all the students join in cleaning their classroom before they go out to play in the playground or to spend free time until afternoon class starts.

Korean children love to play outdoors. After school, teachers of junior classes lead their students out of the school gate. Senior students in elementary schools have more study periods than junior students.

- What is different about the school activities that Korean children do?
- Do you think having a hot lunch at school every day is a good thing? Why or Why not?

Let's Chant

TR 16

1시	2시	3시	4시
han si	du si	se si	ne si

1시	2시	3시	4시	5시	6시
han si	du si	se si	ne si	daseot si	yeoseot si

7시	8시	9시	10시	11시	12시
ilgop si	yeodeol si	ahop si	yeol si	yeolhan si	yeoldu si

Let's Talk

When your partner says the above time and says that he/she is hungry, tell him/her that it is time either for lunch, dinner or a snack.

"12시예요. 배가 고파요."
yeoldusiyeyo   baega gopayo

"점심 시간이에요."
jeomsim siganieyo

Look and Listen 3
TR 16

 7시 반이에요. 뭐 해요?

 아침 먹어요.

8시, 학교에 가요
yeodeolsi   hakgyoe gayo

9시, 공부해요
ahopsi   gongbuhaeyo

12시, 점심 먹어요
yeoldusi   jeomsim meogeoyo

12시 반, 놀아요
yeoldusi ban   norayo

3시, 집에 가요
sesi   jibe gayo

9시, 자요
ahopsi   jayo

••• Let's Talk

Choose a time. Find out what your partner does at that time.

"7시 반이에요. 뭐 해요?"
ilgopsi baniyeyo   mwo haeyo

"아침 먹어요."
achim meogeoyo

•• Let's Role-play

몇 시예요? 뭐 해요?
myeot siyeyo   mwo haeyo

A student stands in front of the class and indicates the time with his/her arm. When the student asks what time it is, the class guesses the time. The student responds to them by saying either "맞아요 (majayo right)" or "틀려요 (teullyeoyo wrong)." The student asks the class what he/she is doing. The student who guesses right stands in front of the class and continues the game.

 TR 16

Listen and Check

Listen carefully to the following words.

1. 놀아요
norayo

2. 먹어요
meogeoyo

3. 자요
jayo

4. 공부해요
gongbuhaeyo

•• Let's Do it Match the picture with the word that is read out.

a. ☐   b. ☐   c. ☐   d. ☐

Let's Review

1. Answer Pepper's question.

지금 몇 시예요?

1)

2)

3)

4)

5)

2. Connect a time with an activity.

1) 아침 7시 반이에요. ●
   achim ilgopsi banieyo

2) 아침 8시예요. ●
   achim yeodeolsiyeyo

3) 저녁 6시예요. ●
   jeonyeok yeoseotsiyeyo

4) 저녁 9시예요. ●
   jeonyeok ahopsiyeyo

● a) 아침 먹어요.
   achim meogeoyo

● b) 저녁 먹어요.
   jeonyeok meogeoyo

● c) 자요.
   jayo

● d) 학교에 가요.
   hakgyoe gayo

3. Complete the sentences with the words in the box.

간식	점심	저녁
gansik	jeomsim	jeonyeok

배가 고파요.

1) 12시예요. _____ 시간이에요.

2) 10시 반이에요. _____ 시간이에요.

3) 6시예요. _____ 시간이에요.

Let's Play a Game "호랑이 아저씨, 몇 시예요?"

horangi ajeossi myeot siyeyo

What's the time, Mr. Tiger?

• **Aim**: To listen accurately to what time other people say and act quickly

• **Method**: The class decides who will act as the tiger. As the tiger moves around, the class follows behind, asking what time it is. The tiger must give the time in sequence, for example, "9시," "10시," "11시," etc. When the tiger says it is time for lunch, a snack or dinner, the class runs away from the tiger who tries to catch them. The one who is caught becomes the tiger and the game continues.

 **Let's Chant**

TR 17

호랑이 아저씨, 몇 시예요?

horangi ajeossi myeot siyeyo

호랑이 아저씨, 몇 시예요?
horangi ajeossi myeot siyeyo

1시예요. 어흥!
hansiyeyo   eoheung

호랑이 아저씨, 몇 시예요?
horangi ajeossi myeot siyeyo

2시예요. 어흥!
dusiyeyo   eoheung

호랑이 아저씨, 몇 시예요?
horangi ajeossi myeot siyeyo

간식 시간이에요!
gansik siganieyo

* This is a variation of a traditional game "What's the time, Mr. Wolf?"

전화 번호가 뭐예요?
What is your telephone number?

Look and Listen 1

TR 18

1	2	3	4	5	6	7	8	9	10
일	이	삼	사	오	육	칠	팔	구	십
il	i	sam	sa	o	yuk	chil	pal	gu	sip

11	12	13	14	15	16	17	18	19	20
십일	십이	십삼	십사	십오	십육	십칠	십팔	십구	이십
sibil	sibi	sipsam	sipsa	sibo	simyuk	sipchil	sippal	sipgu	isip

••• Let's Talk

Ask three people their telephone numbers and write them down.

"전화 번호가 뭐예요?"   "543-1234예요."
jeonhwa beonhoga mwoyeyo   osasame illisamsayeyo

이름	전화번호
	—
	—

••• Let's Talk

Find out the telephone number of your school, teacher and friends.

"학교 전화 번호 알아요?"   "네, 알아요."
hakgyo jeonhwa beonho arayo   ne arayo

"몇 번이에요?"   "425-6780이에요."
myeot beonieyo   saioe yukchilpalgongieyo

••• Let's Do It

Find out the telephone number of a hospital(병원), a library(도서관), a post office(우체국) and a movie theater(영화관). Write the numbers down.

병원 byeongwon	–	우체국 ucheguk	–
도서관 doseogwan	–	영화관 yeonghwagwan	–

Look and Listen 3

생일이
언제예요?

1월 5일
이에요.

			1월			
S	M	T	W	Th	F	S
	1	2	3	4	5	6
7	8	9	10	11	12	13
14	15	16	17	18	19	20
21	22	23	24	25	26	27
28	29	30	31			

1월	2월	3월	4월	5월	6월
irwol	iwol	samwol	sawol	owol	yuwol

7월	8월	9월	10월	11월	12월
chirwol	parwol	guwol	siwol	sibirwol	sibiwol

••• Let's Talk

Find out when the birthdays of three people are and write them down.

"생일이 언제예요?"   "1월 5일이에요."
saengiri eonjeyeyo   irwol oirieyo

이름	생일	
	월	일
	월	일
	월	일

공휴일 National and public holidays
gonghyuil

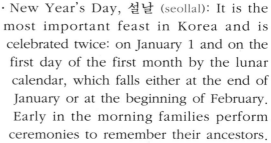

· New Year's Day, 설날 (seollal): It is the most important feast in Korea and is celebrated twice: on January 1 and on the first day of the first month by the lunar calendar, which falls either at the end of January or at the beginning of February. Early in the morning families perform ceremonies to remember their ancestors. Children dress in traditional Korean costume and bow to their parents, grandparents, uncles and aunts. Adults bless children for health and good luck for the year and give them money. After having a big breakfast that includes Korean rice cake soup, 떡국 (tteokguk), younger members of the family visit older relatives to pass on New year's greetings. Family members enjoy playing *yut*, a traditional Korean game.

· March 1 Independent Movement Day: The movement against Japanese rule in 1919

· Buddha's Birthday: This day is celebrated on the eighth day of the fourth month by the lunar calendar. On this day Buddhist temples are packed with people parading with lanterns in the evening.

· May 5 Children's Day 어린이날 (eorininal): Lots of activities are planned for children throughout the country on this day.

· June 6 Memorial Day: Remembering those who fought and died for Korea in war.

· August 15 Liberation Day: Japanese colonial rule over Korea ended in 1945. Japan occupied Korea for 36 years from 1910.

· Autumn Full Moon Day추석 (chuseok): Chuseok is celebrated on the 15th day of the eighth month by the lunar calendar. Families get together to thank their ancestors with newly harvested crops and fruits. On this day Koreans enjoy eating rice cakes called 송편 (songpyeon), which are steamed over pine needles. Memorial ceremonies are also held at family graves.

· October 3 National Foundation Day: The first kingdom of Korea is believed to have been founded by Dangun in 2333 BC.

· December 25 Christmas: Christianity has recently become the most popular religion in Korea.

· May 8 Parents' Day and May 15 Teachers' Day: These days are not holidays. Koreans, however, celebrate these days to show their respect to their parents and teachers in special ways.

· April 5 Arbor Day, July 17 Constitution Day, and October 9 Hangeul Day: These days are not holidays either but the Korean government hold a ceremony to commemorate these days.

- What are two great holidays that every Korean celebrates?
- What kind of special food do Koreans eat on these holidays?
- What is the most important holiday in your country?
- What kind of food do you eat on that holiday?

••• Let's Find Out

생일이 언제예요?
saengiri eonjeyeyo

4월 4일이에요.
sawol sairieyo

설날은 언제예요?
seolnareun eonjeyeyo

1월 1일이에요.
irwol iririeyo

어린이날은 언제예요?
eorininareun eonjeyeyo

5월 5일이에요.
owol oirieyo

Listen and Check

TR 18

Listen carefully to the following words.

1.	2.	3.	4.	5.
3	6	2	10	9
sam	yuk	i	sip	gu

••• **Let's Do it** Enter the number that is read out.

a. ☐   b. ☐   c. ☐   d. ☐   e. ☐

Let's Review

1. Answer Snowy's question.

전화 번호가 뭐예요?

2. Read the telephone numbers of the following places.

학교	hakgyo	329-5188
도서관	doseogwan	432-5678
우체국	ucheguk	710-2345
병원	byeongwon	901-4032

학교 전화 번호는 _____ .
jeonhwa beonhoneun

3. Write down the names of your friends whose birthdays fall into each month shown below.

	이름		이름
1월		7월	
2월		8월	
3월		9월	
4월		10월	
5월		11월	
6월		12월	

4. Fill in the bingo sheet with numbers from 1 to 16. Circle the number that is called. When the circles make a line, four in a row, say "Bingo!" and show the sheet to your partner or teacher.

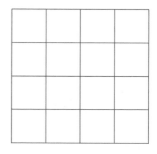

Let's Play a Game "3-6-9, 3-6-9"
sam yuk gu sam yuk gu

- **Aim**: To listen to and count the numbers from 1 except the numbers whose last digit ends in 3, 6 and 9

- **Method**: All the students chant "3-6-9, 3-6-9 (sam-yuk-gu sam-yuk-gu)," After the leader calls out "일 (il 1)," the next person calls out "이 (i 2)." The person in the third position does not call out "삼 (sam 3)," but claps his/her hands. The fourth position calls out "사 (sa 4)." Students who fail to keep the rule are out and the rest of the class starts the game again after chanting "3-6-9, 3-6-9." Those who stay in after five turns of the game are the winners.

Let's Chant

TR 19

3-6-9, 3-6-9
sam yuk gu sam yuk gu

3	6	9	3	6	9
sam	yuk	gu	sam	yuk	gu
3	6	9	3	6	9
sam	yuk	gu	sam	yuk	gu

1 2 ■ 4 5 ■ 7 8 ■ 10 11 12 ■ 14 15 ■ 17 18 ■ 20

3   6   9   13   16   19

* This game was introduced by Mrs. In hee Lee for her own Korean classes.

자 얼마예요?
How much is a ruler?

Look and Listen 1

TR 20

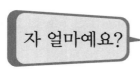

10	20	30	40	50	60	70	80	90
십	이십	삼십	사십	오십	육십	칠십	팔십	구십
sip	isip	samsip	sasip	osip	yuksip	chilsip	palsip	gusip
100	200	300	400	500	600	700	800	900
백	이백	삼백	사백	오백	육백	칠백	팔백	구백
baek								

1,000	2,000
천	이천
cheon	

10,000	20,000
만	이만
man	

가방
gabang
30,000원

모자
moja
9,000원

100,000
십만
simman

1,000,000
백만
baengman

10,000,000
천만
cheonman

차
cha
4,000,000원

집
jip
200,000,000원

100,000,000
억
eok

••• Let's Talk

Point to the items above or to your partner's stationery, and ask him/her how much each item is.

"자 얼마예요?"
ja eolmayeyo

"100원이에요."
baegwonieyo

한국 돈 | Korean money
Hanguk don

Korean money comes in notes and coins in units of *won*. There are three different denominations of notes: 10,000 *won*, 5,000 *won* and 1,000 *won*. King Sejong the Great, 세종대왕 (Sejongdaewang), is printed on green 10,000 *won* notes, 이이 (Yi I), a scholar and minister, is printed on 5,000 *won* notes, and 이황 (Yi Hwang), a great scholar, is printed on 1,000 *won* notes.

At present four different coins are used: 500 *won*, 100 *won*, 50 *won* and 10 *won*. A crane is printed on the 500 *won* coin, 이순신 (Admiral Yi Sun-sin) is printed on the 100 *won* coin, rice plants are on the 50 *won* coin and dabotap, a beautiful pagoda, on the 10 *won* coin.

King Sejong the Great invented the Korean alphabet in 1443 and Admiral Yi Sun-sin defeated the Japanese armada under General Hideyoshi by using turtle ships that he created. The people who are shown on Korean notes and coins are loved and admired for their hard work for Korea.

- Who do you think Koreans love most? Why do you think so?
- How are Korean notes and coins different from those of your country? How are they similar?

Look and Listen 2

사과 10센트
sagwa sip senteu

바나나 20센트
banana isip senteu

우유 1달러 10센트
uyu il dalleo sip senteu

김밥 3달러
gimbap sam dalleo

샌드위치 2달러
saendeuwichi i dalleo

••• Let's Talk

You are buying things from your partner's shop. Point to something of your partner's and ask how much it is.

"주스 주세요. 얼마예요?"   "1달러예요."
juseu juseyo   eolmayeyo   ildalleoyeyo

"여기 있어요."   "고맙습니다."
yeogi isseoyo   gomapseumnida

Look and Listen 3

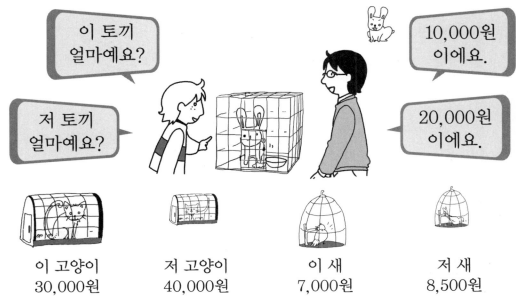

이 토끼 얼마예요?

저 토끼 얼마예요?

10,000원 이에요.

20,000원 이에요.

이 고양이	저 고양이	이 새	저 새
30,000원	40,000원	7,000원	8,500원

• • • **Let's Talk**

Point to things near and far and ask how much they are.

"이 토끼 얼마예요?"
i tokki eolmayeyo

"10,000원이에요."
manwonieyo

"저 토끼 얼마예요?"
jeo tokki eolmayeyo

"20,000원이에요."
imanwonieyo

Listen and Check

Listen carefully to the following words.

1.	2.	3.	4.	5.
99	100	1,000	10,000	50,000
gusipgu	baek	cheon	man	oman

• • • **Let's Do it** Enter the number that is read out.

a. ☐   b. ☐   c. ☐   d. ☐   e. ☐

Let's Review

1. Draw lines to make correct sentences.

1) 지우개는 ●
   jiugaeneun

2) 자는 ●
   janeun

3) 연필은 ●
   yeonpireun

4) 필통은 ●
   piltongeun

● a) 200원이에요.
   ibaegwonieyo

● b) 100원이에요.
   baegwonieyo

● c) 4,000원이에요.
   sacheonwonieyo

● d) 500원이에요.
   obaegwonieyo

얼마예요?

 100원

 200원

 500원

 4,000원

2. Draw lines to connect corresponding responses.

1) 주스 얼마예요? ●
   juseu eolmayeyo

2) 여기 있어요. ●
   yeogi isseoyo

● a) 1달러예요.
   ildalleoyeyo

● b) 고맙습니다.
   gomapseumnida

3. Fill in the blanks with words from the box.

얼마예요	이에요	있어요
eolmayeyo	ieyo	isseoyo

1) A: 고양이 [   ] ?   B: 10,000원이에요.
   goyangi   manwonieyo

2) A: 토끼 얼마예요?   B: 8,000원 [   ] .
   tokki eolmayeyo   palcheonwon

3) A: 고양이 주세요.   B: 여기 [   ] .
   goyangi juseyo   yeogi

Let's Play a Game "고양이 얼마예요?" How much is the cat?
goyangi eolmayeyo

▪ **Aim**: To play "pet shop" using money

▪ **Method**: Lay out some stuffed animals and attach price tags. Divide the class into small groups. Decide who will be the customers, 손님 (sonnim) and who will be the shop owners, 가게 주인 (gage juin). Play the game with Korean money.

손님 sonnim	가게 주인 gage juin
안녕하세요? annyeonghaseyo	어서 오세요. eoseo oseyo
이 고양이 얼마예요? i goyangi eolmayeyo	30,000원이에요. sammanwonieyo
저 고양이 얼마예요? jeo goyangi eolmayeyo	20,000원이에요. imanwonieyo
이 고양이를 좋아해요. i goyangireul joahaeyo	
이 고양이 주세요. i goyangi juseyo	여기 있어요. yeogi isseoyo
30,000원 여기 있어요. sammanwon yeogi isseoyo	고맙습니다. gomapseumnida
안녕히 계세요. annyeonghi gyeseyo	안녕히 가세요. annyeonghi gaseyo

물고기 mulgogi 1,000원	새 sae 5,000원	토끼 tokki 10,000원	다람쥐 daramjwi 3,000원	개 gae 40,000원

* Use stationery goods intead of stuffed animals, keeping all the other rules the same.

아나는 키가 커요.
Ana is tall.

Look and Listen 1

TR 21

아나(Ana)는 키가 커요.
머리가 길어요.

빌리는 눈이 커요.
코가 작아요.
입이 커요.

팀은 키가 작아요.
머리가 짧아요.

••• **Let's Talk**

Take turns telling your partner how he/she looks.

"아나는 키가 커요. 머리가 길어요."
ananeun kiga keoyo   meoriga gireoyo

"팀은 키가 작아요. 머리가 짧아요."
timeun kiga jagayo   meoriga jjalbayo

"빌리는 눈이 커요. 코가 작아요. 입이 커요."
billineun nuni keoyo   koga jagayo   ibi keoyo

Look and Listen2

소는 커요.

곰도 커요.

기린은 목이 길어요.

쥐는 작아요.

닭도 작아요.

코끼리는 코가 길어요.

••• Let's Talk

Point to the animals above and talk about how they look.

"소는 커요."
soneun keoyo

"쥐는 작아요."
jwineun jagayo

"기린은 목이 길어요."
girineun mogi gireoyo

"곰도 커요."
gomdo keoyo

"닭도 작아요."
dakdo jagayo

"코끼리는 코가 길어요."
kokkirineun koga gireoyo

Look and Listen 3

•• **Let's Talk**

Point to the animals above and talk about how they look.

"아나는 예뻐요. 날씬해요."　"이안은 멋있어요."
ananeun yeppeoyo　nalssinhaeyo　　ianeun meosisseoyo

"하마는 뚱뚱해요."　"원숭이도 뚱뚱해요?"　"아니요, 보통이에요."
hamaneun ttungttunghaeyo　wonsungido ttungttunghaeyo　aniyo botongieyo

띠
tti

The cycle of twelve animals

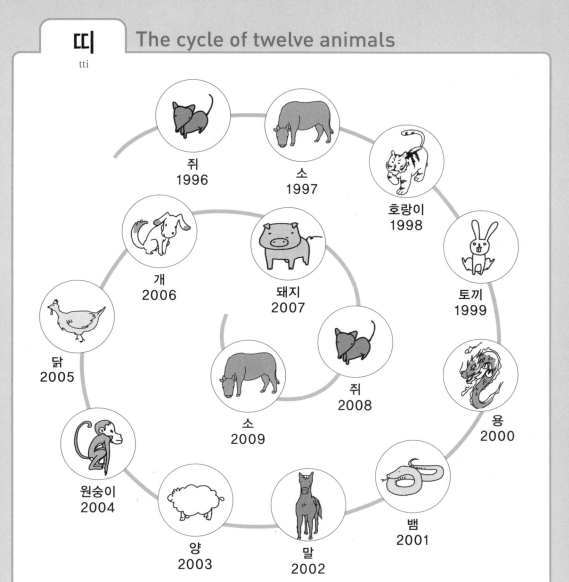

쥐
1996

소
1997

호랑이
1998

토끼
1999

용
2000

뱀
2001

말
2002

양
2003

원숭이
2004

닭
2005

개
2006

돼지
2007

쥐
2008

소
2009

Since long ago Koreans have used a twelve-animal cycle to represent hours and years. The cycle begins with the mouse and ends with the pig. Even today, Koreans say that the year 2009 is the Year of Ox. All the Korean babies born in 2009 carry their birth year and are called ox-year people, 소 띠 (so tti). Those who are born twelve years before, in 1997, are also 소 띠 (so tti). The twelve animals and their corresponding years are shown above.

- Which animal year is this year?
- Can you work out which animal year your year of birth is?

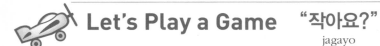

Let's Play a Game "작아요?" Is it small?
jagayo

▪ **Aim**: To guess the animal acted out by other groups by asking questions

▪ **Method**: Divide the class into three groups. Each group decides which animal the group will act. Members of one group express the animal through actions. Other groups guess in turn which animal this group is by asking questions about its appearance, as listed below. The answers can be one of three responses only: "네 (ne)," "아니요 (aniyo)" and "보통이에요 (botongieyo)." The group that makes the right guess is the winner.

질문 Questions		대답 Answers
작아요? jagayo	뚱뚱해요? ttungttunghaeyo	네. ne
키가 커요? kiga keoyo	소예요? soyeyo	아니요. aniyo
코가 길어요? koga gireoyo	하마예요? hamayeyo	보통이에요. botongieyo

TR 21

Listen and Check

Listen carefully to the following words.

1. 커요
keoyo

2. 작아요
jagayo

3. 길어요
gireoyo

4. 짧아요
jjalbayo

5. 뚱뚱해요
ttungttunghaeyo

••• **Let's Do it** Match the picture with the word that is read out.

a. ☐   b. ☐   c. ☐   d. ☐   e. ☐

1. Fill in the blanks by selecting the right words.

커요	작아요	길어요
keoyo	jagayo	gireoyo

1) 키가 [   ]

2) 머리가 [   ]

3) 입이 [   ]

4) 키가 [   ]

2. Draw lines to connect the animals with their appearances.

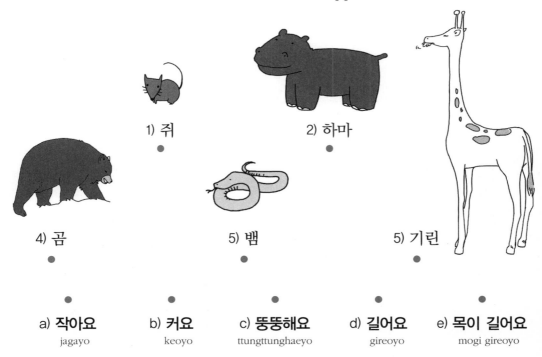

1) 쥐

2) 하마

4) 곰

5) 뱀

5) 기린

a) **작아요**
jagayo

b) **커요**
keoyo

c) **뚱뚱해요**
ttungttunghaeyo

d) **길어요**
gireoyo

e) **목이 길어요**
mogi gireoyo

Unit 12

무슨 색을 좋아해요?
What color do you like?

Look and Listen 1

TR 22

까만
머리예요.

노란 바나나
noran banana

빨간 사과
ppalgan sagwa

파란 하늘
paran haneul

하얀 머리
hayan meori

••• Let's Talk

Talk about the color of your friends' hair.

"까만 머리예요."
kkaman meoriyeyo

Let's Chant

TR 22

무지개
mujigae

빨	주	노	초	파	남	보
ppal	ju	no	cho	pa	nam	bo
빨	주	노	초	파	남	보
ppal	ju	no	cho	pa	nam	bo
빨	주	노	초	파	남	보
ppal	ju	no	cho	pa	nam	bo

Look and Listen 2

TR 22

무슨 색을 좋아해요?

파란색을 좋아해요.

파란색 주세요.

노란색	주황색	빨간색	초록색
noransaek	juhwangsaek	ppalgansaek	choroksaek

남색	보라색	갈색
namsaek	borasaek	galsaek

••• Let's Talk

When asked what color you like, answer and then ask for it.

"무슨 색을 좋아해요?"
museun saegeul joahaeyo

"파란색을 좋아해요. 파란색 주세요."
paransaegeul joahaeyo   paransaek juseyo

Let's Chant

TR 23

나미 저고리
nami jeogori

나미 저고리
nami jeogori

나미 저고리
nami jeogori

분홍 저고리
bunhong jeogori

나미 저고리
nami jeogori

••• Let's Do it

Color in the pictures of 태극기 (taegeukgi), 무궁화 (mugunghwa), and 한복 (hanbok).

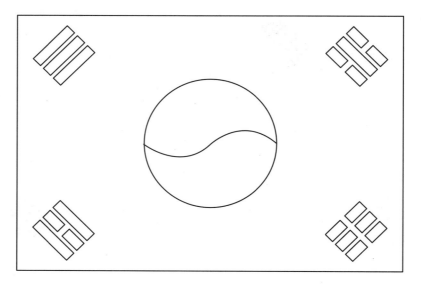

태극기
taegeukgi

무궁화
mugunghwa

한복
hanbok

Listen and Check

Listen carefully to the following words.

1.

노란 바나나
noran banana

2.

빨간 사과
ppalgan sagwa

3.

파란 하늘
paran haneul

••• **Let's Do it** Match the picture with the word that is read out.

a. ☐   b. ☐   c. ☐

1. Answer Pepper's questions.

1) 바나나는 무슨 색이에요?
banananeun museun saegieyo

[ ] 색이에요.

2) 사과는 무슨 색이에요?
sagwaneun museun saegieyo

[ ] 색이에요.

3) 나미 머리는 무슨 색이에요?
nami meorineun museun saegieyo

[ ] 색이에요.

빨간	까만	노란
ppalgan	kkaman	noran

2. Answer the questions.

1) 보라색을 좋아해요?
borasaegeul joahaeyo

[ ] (네. / 아니요.)

2) 초록색을 좋아해요?
choroksaegeul joahaeyo

[ ] (네. / 아니요.)

3) 분홍색을 좋아해요?
bunhongsaegeul joahaeyo

[ ] (네. / 아니요.)

4) 무슨 색을 좋아해요?
museun saegeul joahaeyo

[ ] 색을 좋아해요.

3. Complete the following by filling in the spaces and then add them to your chants.

나미 저고리
나미 저고리
[ ] 저고리
나미 저고리

[ ] 지우개
[ ] 지우개
[ ] 지우개
[ ] 지우개

Let's Play a Game "파란색 어디 있어요?" Where are you, Blue?
paransaek eodi isseoyo

▪ **Aim**: To bring members of the other group to your group by calling out for the colors that students wear or hold

▪ **Method**: Divide the class into two groups. Each group looks at the colors which the other group members are wearing or holding in their hands and decide which color to call out. After group A chants or sings the first line, calling out a certain color, group B members who are wearing or holding the color come out chanting or singing and join group A. group B takes their turn and chants or sings the first line. The group who has more members remaining after doing this five times is the winner.

TR 24

Let's Sing "파란색, 파란색, 어디 있어요?"
paransaek paransaek eodi isseoyo

파란색, 파란색, 어디 있어요?
paransaek paransaek eodi isseoyo

여기 있어요. 여기 있어요. 안녕하세요!
yeogi isseoyo   yeogi isseoyo   annyeonghaseyo

노란색, 노란색, 어디 있어요?
noransaek noransaek eodi isseoyo

여기 있어요. 여기 있어요. 안녕하세요!
yeogi isseoyo   yeogi isseoyo   annyeonghaseyo

＊ Variation: Students can hold flash cards with the words of a color instead of using colored items.

APPENDIX

Checklist

Unit 01

Before the lesson, see if you have the following items ready:

☐   photographs of your family

☐   pictures of people whom you like, such as singers and actors

After the lesson, check whether you can:

☐   ask who the person at the door is.

☐   welcome the visitor.

☐   ask your friends who the person next to them (younger/older than you) is.

☐   introduce your family, friends or favorite people to your classmates.

Unit 02

Before the lesson, see if you have the following items ready:

☐   pictures of a group of people

☐   pictures of birthday cakes with candles on it

After the lesson, check whether you can:

☐   count how many people are in the pictures or in the classroom.

☐   guess the age of the birthday person by counting the candles.

☐   ask your friends' age and tell how old you are.

Unit 03

Before the lesson, see if you have the following items ready:

☐   pictures of people of different nationalities

☐   ask people to speak and then to be quiet

After the lesson, check whether you can:

☐   ask people where they come from.

☐   tell others where you and the people in the pictures come from.

☐   read and write words with ㄷ[d], ㄹ[r/l], ㅡ[eo], ㅗ[o] and ㅛ[yo].

Unit 04

Before the lesson, see if you have the following items ready:

☐   puppets or stuffed animals

After the lesson, check whether you can:

☐   ask people how they are doing.

☐   tell others which part of you or your stuffed animals' body hurts.

☐   say goodbye to visitors.

Unit 05

Before the lesson, see if you have the following items ready:

☐   pictures of places and/or brochures for tourists

After the lesson, check whether you can:

☐   ask people where they are going.
☐   suggest going somewhere together with others.
☐   tell others where exactly you are going.

Unit 06

Before the lesson, see if you have the following items ready:

☐   photographs of your pets
☐   pictures of animals that you like or dislike

After the lesson, check whether you can:

☐   ask people whether they like a certain animal.
☐   ask people whether they have a certain animal.
☐   ask people whether they are looking for a certain animal.

Unit 07

Before the lesson, see if you have the following items ready:

☐   pictures or a list of sports that you like to play

After the lesson, check whether you can:

☐   ask people whether they play a certain sport.
☐   ask people what sports they play.
☐   ask people whether they like a certain outdoor activity.

Unit 08

Before the lesson, see if you have the following items ready:

☐   your daily timetable

After the lesson, check whether you can:

☐   ask what time it is.
☐   say what time it is.
☐   talk about your timetable.

Checklist

Unit 09

Before the lesson, see if you have the following items ready:

☐ telephone numbers that you frequently dial

After the lesson, check whether you can:

☐ ask what others' telephone numbers are.
☐ say what your own telephone number is.
☐ find out the telephone numbers of places that you frequently visit.
☐ ask when others' birthdays are and talk about your birthday.

Unit 10

Before the lesson, see if you have the following items ready:

☐ coins and small notes

After the lesson, check whether you can:

☐ find out how much things cost.
☐ use Korean money to buy small things.

Unit 11

Before the lesson, see if you have the following items ready:

☐ stuffed animals which have long, short, big or small body parts

After the lesson, check whether you can:

☐ talk about how people look.
☐ talk about the characters of animals.

Unit 12

Before the lesson, see if you have the following items ready:

☐ pieces of paper in different colors
☐ favorite things with bright colors

After the lesson, check whether you can:

☐ talk about things with bright colors.
☐ ask others which color(s) they like.

Answers

Unit 01

Listen and Check p.16

a. 3   b. 4   c. 1   d. 2   e. 5

Let's Review p.17

1. 1) 할아버지   2) 외할머니   3) 어머니
   4) 오빠   5) 여동생

2. 1) 학생
   2) 루치아노 파바로티예요, 오페라 가수예요
   3) 니콜 키드먼이에요, 영화 배우예요

Unit 02

Listen and Check p.23

a. 1   b. 3   c. 5   d. 4   e. 2

Let's Review p.24

2. 1) a   2) b   3) c

Unit 03

Listen and Check p.28

a. 1   b. 4   c. 5   d. 2   e. 3

Let's Review p.30

2. 1) c   2) b   3) a

3. 1) 아프리카   2) 호주
   3) 영국   4) 캐나다

Unit 04

Listen and Check p.36

a. 3   b. 1   c. 4   d. 2

Let's Review p.37

1. 1) a   2) c   3) b

Unit 05

Listen and Check p.43

a. 4   b. 1   c. 2   d. 3

Let's Review p.44

2. 1) 공원

4. 1) a   2) b

Unit 06

Listen and Check p.48

a.1   b. 3   c. 4   d. 2   e. 5

Let's Review p.52

1. 1) c   2) a   3) b   4) d

Answers

Unit 07

Listen and Check p.57

a. 4   b. 2   c. 1   d. 3

Let's Review p.58

2. 1) b   2) a   3) d   4) c

3. 1) 야구해요   2) 테니스해요
   3) 농구해요   4) 골프해요
   5) 축구해요

Unit 08

Listen and Check p.64

a. 3   b. 4   c. 1   d. 2

Let's Review p.65

3. 1) 두 시예요.   2) 다섯 시예요.
   3) 열두 시예요.   4) 세 시예요.
   5) 여덟 시예요.

2. 1) a   2) d   3) b   4) c

3. 1) 점심   2) 간식   3) 저녁

Unit 09

Listen and Check p.71

a. 1   b. 2   c. 5   d. 4   e. 3

Let's Review p.72

2. 학교 전화 번호는 삼이구에 오일팔팔이에요.
   도서관 전화 번호는 사삼이에 오육칠팔이에요.
   우체국 전화 번호는 칠일공에 이삼사오예요.
   병원 전화 번호는 구공일에 사공삼이에요.

Unit 10

Listen and Check p.77

a. 2   b. 4   c. 3   d. 5   e. 1

Let's Review p.78

1. 1) b   2) a   3) d   4) c

2. 1) a   2) b

3. 1) 얼마예요   2) 이에요   3) 있어요

Unit 11

Listen and Check p.84

a. 5   b. 2   c. 4   d. 3   e. 1

Let's Review p.85

1. 1) 커요   2) 길어요
   3) 커요   4) 작아요

2. 1) a   2) c   3) b   4) d   5) e

Unit 12

Listen and Check p.89

a. 1   b. 3   c. 2

Let's Review p.90

1. 1) 노란   2) 빨간   3) 까만

List of Words and Phrases

Unit 01 누구예요?

누구	nugu	who
어서 오세요	eoseo oseyo	welcome (as a formal greeting)
가족	gajok	family
할아버지	harabeoji	grandfather
할머니	halmeoni	grandmother
외할아버지	oeharabeoji	grandfather (on mother's side)
외할머니	oehalmeoni	grandmother (on mother's side)
아버지 / 아빠	abeoji/appa	father
어머니 / 엄마	eomeoni/eomma	mother
언니	eonni	older sister (for girls)
오빠	oppa	older brother (for girls)
여동생	yeodongsaeng	younger sister
남동생	namdongsaeng	younger brother
얘	yae	this kid/person
동생	dongsaeng	younger brother or sister
주디	judi	Judy
팀	tim	Tim
친구	chingu	friend
빌리	billi	Billy
이분	ibun	this person (very polite)
−은/−는	eun/neun	topic marker
사진	sajin	photograph
누나	nuna	older sister (for boys)
형	hyeong	older brother (for boys)
존	jon	John
제인	jein	Jane
줄리아	jullia	Julia
마이클	maikeul	Michael
−하고	hago	and

List of Words and Phrases

Unit 01 누구예요?

학생	haksaeng	student
나라	nara	country
루치아노 파바로티	ruchiano pabaroti	Luciano Pavarotti
니콜 키드먼	nikol kideumeon	Nicole Kidman
오페라	opera	opera
가수	gasu	singer
영화	yeonghwa	movie
배우	baeu	actor/actress
맞았어요.	majasseoyo	(You) have done it right./You're right.
잘 했어요.	jal haesseoyo	(You) have done it well./Good work.
틀렸어요.	teullyeosseoyo	(You) have done it wrong./You're wrong.
다시	dasi	again
한 번	han beon	once
해 보세요.	hae boseyo	Please try (doing it).

Unit 02 몇 살이에요?

몇	myeot	how many, what
살	sal	counting stem for age
하나	hana	1
둘	dul	2
셋	set	3
넷	net	4
다섯	daseot	5
여섯	yeoseot	6
일곱	ilgop	7
여덟	yeodeol	8
아홉	ahop	9

Unit 02 몇 살이에요?

열	yeol	10
열하나	yeolhana	11
열둘	yeoldul	12
열셋	yeolset	13
열넷	yeollet	14
열다섯	yeoldaseot	15
열여섯	yeollyeoseot	16
열일곱	yeorilgop	17
열여덟	yeollyeodeol	18
열아홉	yeorahop	19
스물	seumul	20
서른	seoreun	30
마흔	maheun	40
쉰	swin	50
예순	yesun	60
일흔	ilheun	70
여든	yeodeun	80
아흔	aheun	90
백	baek	100
생일	saengil	birthday
돌	dol	first birthday
환갑	hwangap	60th birthday
축하합니다.	chukhahamnida	Congratulations.
사랑하는	saranghaneun	dear, beloved
명	myeong	counter for person
남학생	namhaksaeng	boy student
여학생	yeohaksaeng	girl student
꼬마	kkoma	little child
인디안	indian	Indian

List of Words and Phrases

Unit 03 어디에서 왔어요?

–에서	eseo	from
왔어요	wasseoyo	(I) have come
러시아	reosia	Russia
네덜란드	nedeollandeu	Netherlands
독일	dogil	Germany
프랑스	peurangseu	France
스페인	seupein	Spain
이탈리아	itallia	Italy
인도	indo	India
베트남	beteunam	Vietnam
필리핀	pillipin	Philippines
말레이시아	malleisia	Malaysia
싱가포르	singgaporeu	Singapore
인도네시아	indonesia	Indonesia
남아프리카공화국	namapeurika gonghwaguk	the Republic of South Africa
부산	busan	Busan
인천	incheon	Incheon
광주	gwangju	Gwangju
대구	daegu	Daegu
대전	daejeon	Daejeon
수원	suwon	Suwon
평양	pyeongyang	Pyeongyang
베이징	beijing	Beijing
워싱턴	wosingteon	Washington
캔버라	kaenbeora	Canberra
웰링턴	wellingteon	Wellington
싱가포르	singgaporeu	Singapore
동대문	dongdaemun	East Gate
남대문	namdaemun	South Gate
경복궁	gyeongbokgung	Gyeongbokgung Palace
세종대왕	sejongdaewang	King Sejong the Great

Unit 03 어디에서 왔어요?

한강	hangang	Han River
팬더	paendeo	panda
똑똑	ttokttok	knock-knock
버팔로	beopallo	buffalo

Unit 04 어떻게 지내요?

어떻게	eotteoke	how
지내요	jinaeyo	get on
그저 그래요.	geujeo geuraeyo	(I am) so, so.
아파요.	apayo	(I'm) hurt./(I'm) in pain.
머리	meori	head, hair
-가/-이	ga/i	subject marker
눈	nun	eye
어깨	eokkae	shoulder
무릎	mureup	knee
발	bal	foot
배	bae	tummy, stomach
-도	do	as well, also
안	an	not
코	ko	nose
귀	gwi	ear
입	ip	mouth
목	mok	neck
손	son	hand
팔	pal	arm
다리	dari	leg
의사	uisa	doctor
환자	hwanja	patient
안녕히 계세요.	annyeonghi gyeseyo	Goodbye. (Stay in peace.)
안녕히 가세요.	annyeonghi gaseyo	Goodbye. (Go in peace.)

List of Words and Phrases

많이	mani	a lot
쉬세요.	swiseyo	Please have a rest.

Unit 05 어디에 가요?

−에	e	to
가요	gayo	(I) go
가게	gage	shop
병원	byeongwon	hospital
공원	gongwon	park
같이	gachi	together
우체국	ucheguk	post office
영화관	yeonghwagwan	movie theater
교회	gyohoe	church
동물원	dongmurwon	zoo
샌프란시스코	saenpeuransiseuko	San Francisco
로스앤젤리스	roseuaenjellis	Los Angeles
시카고	sikago	Chicago
토론토	toronto	Toronto
밴쿠버	baenkubeo	Vancouver
크라이스트처치	keuraiseuteucheochi	Christchurch
던이든	deonideun	Dunedin
멜번	melbeon	Melbourne
브리스번	beuriseubeon	Brisbane
퍼스	peoseu	Perth

Unit 06 개를 좋아해요?

−를/−을	reul/eul	object marker
좋아해요	joahaeyo	(I) like
마리	mari	counting unit for animals
고양이	goyangi	cat

Unit 06 개를 좋아해요?

토끼	tokki	rabbit
물고기	mulgogi	fish
뱀	baem	snake
싫어해요	sireohaeyo	(I) dislike
거미	geomi	spider
파리	pari	fly
모기	mogi	mosquito
야옹	yaong	meow
멍멍	meong-meong	bow-wow
매애	maeae	baa
음매	eummae	moo
다람쥐	daramjwi	squirrel
찾아요	chajayo	(I) search for, find
곰	gom	bear
단군	dangun	Dangun

Unit 07 수영해요?

수영해요	suyeonghaeyo	(I) swim
해요	haeyo	(I) do
축구	chukgu	soccer
야구	yagu	baseball
농구	nonggu	basketball
배구	baegu	volleyball
탁구	takgu	table tennis
럭비	reokbi	rugby
테니스	teniseu	tennis
무슨	museun	what kind of
운동	undong	sports
태권도	taegwondo	taegwondo
하키	haki	hockey

List of Words and Phrases

Unit 07 수영해요?

넷볼	netbol	netball
골프	golpeu	golf
캠핑	kaemping	camping
말타기	maltagi	horse riding
낚시	naksi	fishing
달리기	dalligi	running
스키	seuki	ski
박찬호	bak chan ho	Chan-ho Park
앙드레 아가시	angdeure agasi	Andre Agassi
마이클 조던	maikeul jodeon	Michael Jordan
타이거 우즈	taigeo ujeu	Tiger Woods
데이비드 베컴	deibideu bekeom	David Beckham

Unit 08 지금 몇 시예요?

지금	jigeum	now
시	si	time
배가 고파요.	baega gopayo	(I am) hungry.
점심	jeomsim	lunch
시간	sigan	hour, time
반	ban	half
간식	gansik	snack
저녁	jeonyeok	dinner, evening
아침	achim	breakfast, morning
먹어요.	meogeoyo	(I) eat.
공부해요.	gongbuhaeyo	(I) study.
놀아요.	norayo	(I) play.
자요.	jayo	(I) sleep.
아저씨	ajeossi	uncle (or any man of marrying age)

Unit 09 전화 번호가 뭐예요?

전화	jeonhwa	telephone
번호	beonho	number
일	il	1
이	i	2
삼	sam	3
사	sa	4
오	o	5
육	yuk	6
칠	chil	7
팔	pal	8
구	gu	9
십	sip	10
십일	sibil	11
십이	sibi	12
십삼	sipsam	13
십사	sipsa	14
십오	sibo	15
십육	simyuk	16
십칠	sipchil	17
십팔	sippal	18
십구	sipgu	19
이십	isip	20
알아요	arayo	know
언제	eonje	when
월	wol	month
일	il	day
1월	irwol	January
2월	iwol	February
3월	samwol	March
4월	sawol	April
5월	owol	May

List of Words and Phrases

Unit 09 전화 번호가 뭐예요?

6월	yuwol	June
7월	chirwol	July
8월	parwol	August
9월	guwol	September
10월	siwol	October
11월	sibirwol	November
12월	sibiwol	December
설날	seollal	New Year's Day
어린이날	eorininal	Children's Day
추석	chuseok	Autumn Full Moon Day

Unit 10 자 얼마예요?

얼마	eolma	how much
삼십	samsip	30
사십	sasip	40
오십	osip	50
육십	yuksip	60
칠십	chilsip	70
팔십	palsip	80
구십	gusip	90
백	baek	100
이백	ibaek	200
천	cheon	1,000
이천	icheon	2,000
만	man	10,000
이만	iman	20,000
십만	simman	100,000
이십만	isimman	200,000
백만	baengman	1,000,000
천만	cheonman	10,000,000

Unit 10 자 얼마예요?

억	eok	100,000,000
돈	don	money
이순신	yi sun sin	Admiral Yi Sun-sin
달러	dalleo	dollar
센트	senteu	cent
김밥	gimbap	seaweed rolls
샌드위치	saendeuwichi	sandwich
이	i	this
저	jeo	that
손님	sonnim	customer, visitor
주인	juin	owner, master

Unit 11 아나는 키가 커요.

키	ki	height
키가 커요.	kiga keoyo	(I'm) tall.
키가 작아요.	kiga jagayo	(I'm) short.
길어요.	gireoyo	(It's) long.
짧아요.	jjalbayo	(It's) short.
커요.	keoyo	(It's) big.
작아요.	jagayo	(It's) small.
쥐	jwi	mouse
닭	dak	chicken
기린	girin	giraffe
예뻐요.	yebbeoyo	(It's) pretty.
날씬해요.	nalssinhaeyo	(I'm) thin.
멋있어요.	meosisseoyo	(I'm) charming, good-looking.
하마	hama	hippopotamus
뚱뚱해요.	ttungttunghaeyo	(I'm) fat.
보통이에요.	botongieyo	(It's) average.

List of Words and Phrases

Unit 11 아나는 키가 커요.

용	yong	dragon
띠	tti	the cycle of twelve animals

Unit 12 무슨 색을 좋아해요?

까만	kkaman	black
노란	noran	yellow
빨간	bbalgan	red
파란	paran	blue
하늘	haneul	sky
하얀	hayan	white
무지개	mujigae	rainbow
색	saek	color
주황	juhwang	orange
초록	chorok	green
남색	namsaek	indigo
보라	bora	violet
갈색	galsaek	brown
분홍	bunhong	pink

The Sounds of the Korean Alphabet

Fourteen basic consonant letters

letter	sounds similar to the bold letter	can be written as
ㄱ	green / cook*	g, k ^
ㄴ	name	n
ㄷ	dance / * top	d, t ^
ㄹ	rake / reel	r, l ^^
ㅁ	make	m
ㅂ	bread / hop*	b, p ^
ㅅ	*sand	s
ㅇ	song**	[ ], ng
ㅈ	*juice	j
ㅊ	chop	ch
ㅋ	kite	k
ㅌ	top	t
ㅍ	pen	p
ㅎ	hope	h

Other consonant letters

letter	sounds similar to the bold letter	can be written as
ㄲ	skin	kk
ㄸ	still	tt
ㅃ	spin	pp
ㅆ	sand	ss
ㅉ	pizza	jj

* Say this without a strong puff of air.

** Before a vowel, ㅇ does not make any sound. In the final position after a vowel, however, it sounds like the last part of "sing" or "song."

^ Before a vowel or between vowels, ㄱ, ㄷ and ㅂ are written as "g, d and b." Before a consonant, they are usually written as "k, t and p." At the end of a word, they are always written as "k, t and p."

^^ Before a vowel or between vowels, ㄹ is written as "r." Before a consonant or at the end of a word, ㄹ is written as "l." ㄹㄹ is written as "ll."

The Sounds of the Korean Alphabet

Ten basic vowel letters

letter	sounds similar to the bold letter	can be written as
ㅏ	**fa**ther	a
ㅑ	**ya**hoo	ya
ㅓ	**a**go	eo
ㅕ	**you**ng	yeo
ㅗ	**o**pen	o
ㅛ	**yo**ga	yo
ㅜ	s**oo**n	u
ㅠ	**you**	yu
ㅡ	p**u**ll *	eu
ㅣ	f**ee**t	i

Other vowel letters

letter	sounds similar to the bold letter	can be written as
ㅐ	c**a**t	ae
ㅒ	**Ya**nkee	yae
ㅔ	p**e**n	e
ㅖ	**ye**s	ye
ㅘ	Ha**wa**ii	wa
ㅙ	**wa**x	wae
ㅚ	**we**t	oe
ㅝ	**wa**ter	wo
ㅞ	**we**t	we
ㅟ	**we**	wi
ㅢ	**	ui

* No lip rounding.

** No matching sound in English. Say ㅡ and ㅣ quickly one after the other.